THE POLAR EXPRESS
THE MOVIE

The MOVIE SCRAPBOOK

WRITTEN
BY
MELISSA MORGAN AND HEIDI CHO

BASED ON THE MOTION PICTURE SCREENPLAY
BY
ROBERT ZEMECKIS AND WILLIAM BROYLES, JR.

BASED ON THE BOOK *THE POLAR EXPRESS*,

WRITTEN AND ILLUSTRATED
BY
CHRIS VANN ALLSBURG

DESIGN
BY
DOYLE PARTNERS

■SCHOLASTIC

Scholastic Children's Books
Commonwealth House, 1-19 New Oxford Street
London WC1A 1NU, UK
a division of Scholastic Ltd
London ~ New York ~ Toronto ~ Sydney ~ Auckland
Mexico City ~ New Delhi ~ Hong Kong

First published in the USA by Houghton Mifflin Company, 2004
First published in paperback in the UK by Scholastic Ltd, 2004

ISBN 0 439 95913 6

Printed by Proost, Belgium

2 4 6 8 10 9 7 5 3 1

Late one Christmas Eve, many years ago, a young boy was awoken by the sound of a train hissing to a halt outside his bedroom window. The train was the *Polar Express*, which waited to take the boy on a journey to the North Pole. The boy had been specially chosen for the trip so that he could search for answers to his questions about Santa Claus. During this trip the boy met people and saw places that filled his eyes with wonder and excitement, and taught him valuable lessons of friendship and faith. Most importantly, the journey to the North Pole gave the boy a chance to believe in the magic of Christmas again.

This is a scrapbook of the boy's memories of his adventure that one enchanted night, many years ago.

BALDWIN LOCOMOTIVE WORKS

One of the most famous and successful steam locomotive manufacturers in the world was called Baldwin Locomotive Works of Philadelphia. Baldwin was the largest locomotive builder in the nineteenth century. Baldwin was well known for its incredibly fast production rates – a single engine took the factory only eight weeks to build from beginning to end. How was it possible for Baldwin to produce their magnificent steamers at such unbelievable speed?

The secret was in the many thousands of workers employed to make the most magnificent steam engines around. It was the extraordinary work of specialists like blacksmiths, drillers, pipe fitters, draftsmen, painters and machinists who all came together in the final stages of fitting together each locomotive. In fact, the frames and machined parts built by these craftsmen were made so precisely that, inside an erecting shop the size of an entire city block, it took an army of 3,200 workers only one week to fit together all the parts! At that rate it's no surprise that the company, established in 1831, built about 75,000 locomotives from the day it opened until it closed its doors in 1956.

POLAR EXPRESS

You might take **trains** for granted, but they're only about 200 years old!

THE STEAM LOCOMOTIVE

In 1804 the invention of the locomotive changed the way people lived. This new 'speedy' train travel made it possible for people to live much further from their workplaces, and to visit faraway places in a much shorter period of time. And because the trains carried goods as well as people, it became possible to buy things like fresh fruit and vegetables far from where they were grown!

One of the first locomotives to be built for the transportation of commercial goods was called the *Rocket*, and it travelled at 29 miles per hour. That may not sound very fast to us now, but remember that before these early trains were invented, the fastest way for groups to travel was in a carriage pulled by mules or horses! In fact, this high-speed train travel was once considered so technologically advanced that one scientist thought that the speed could make people's brains fall out!

THE ROCKET.

The Christmas stocking tradition

THE LEGEND OF THE CHRISTMAS STOCKING

Once upon a time there was a very kind but poor nobleman who had three daughters. When it was time for his daughters to marry, the nobleman became very unhappy because he didn't have enough money to provide dowries for their weddings. One night, after the daughters had washed their clothing, they hung their stockings over the fireplace as usual to dry, and went off to bed. That same night, Christmas Eve, while the family was sleeping, Saint Nicholas peered into the window and saw the daughters' stockings hanging by the fire. Knowing the despair of their father, Saint Nicholas took three small bags of gold from his pouch and threw them carefully, one by one, down the chimney and into the drying stockings. The next morning when the daughters awoke, they each found enough gold for them to get married. The whole family was overjoyed, and a new Christmas tradition was born!

Children all over the world continue the tradition of hanging Christmas stockings or practise similar customs. In France and Scandinavia, kids place their shoes by the fireplace in hope of finding them filled with goodies on Christmas Day. Children in Hungary even polish their shoes so they will be shiny before setting them out near the door or on a window sill, hoping to find them filled with treats in the morning!

It's snowing! It's snowing!

DO YOU KNOW THAT IF YOU STICK OUT YOUR TONGUE TO CATCH A SNOWFLAKE, YOU'RE PROBABLY EATING DUST?

That's right! Almost every snowflake that falls starts off as a tiny speck of dust swirling around high in the sky. When the dust speck flies deep inside a cloud, water vapour clings to it and freezes, holding fast. This icy fleck then starts to bump into other frozen crystals, and they freeze together, forming bigger crystals. Each snowflake is made up from two to two hundred separate ice crystals. When the flake becomes heavy enough, it ends its long journey by floating softly to the ground. There, it can become part of a fort, a snowball, or even a snowman!

PROJECT

Do you believe that no two
snowflakes are alike?
See for yourself!

1. All you need to catch some falling
snowflakes is a strip of dark fabric that's
been out in the cold for ten minutes (so
the snowflakes won't melt when they land).

2. During the next snowfall, go outside
and hold the fabric taut. Catch as many
snowflakes as you can, then use a magnifying
glass to examine them. Notice the variety of
unique, beautiful patterns you've captured.

3. If you want, you can sketch the shapes
into a notebook and compare the patterns to
see how they're similar and how they're
different!

Snowflakes might be good at sticking together,
but each is definitely one of a kind. No two
snowflakes look exactly the same — each one has
six sides but is beautiful and unique with its
own special design. The shape that a flake will
be depends on the temperature that it forms in!
The colder it is outside, the smaller and more
intricately patterned the snowflake will be.

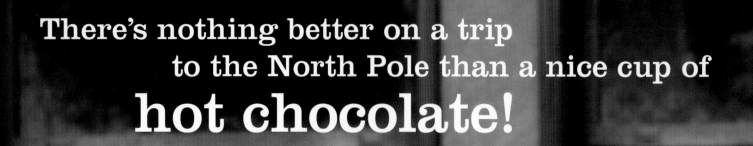

There's nothing better on a trip to the North Pole than a nice cup of hot chocolate!

THE POLAR EXPRESS
HOT CHOCOLATE

PER PORTION

1 generous cup of milk
1 very generous teaspoon of chocolate
(powdered or syrup)

ON THE HOB

Add ingredients to a saucepan
and heat on low, stirring until steam rises.
(Ask an adult to help you. Do not overheat.)

Pour into a mug.

IN A MICROWAVE

Pour ingredients into a mug.

Heat and stir.
(Ask an adult to help you. Do not overheat.)

For a Christmas treat, add a marshmallow or
cinnamon stick when serving. Enjoy!

WHEN HOT CHOCOLATE WAS REALLY HOT

The Aztecs, an ancient Mexican civilization, used to make their 'hot' chocolate cold and flavoured with wine and hot chilli peppers! Imagine what that tasted like! That was the first form of chocolate ever discovered by Europeans, and that's the way it was introduced to Spain in the early 1500s by the explorer Hernan Cortes.

The Spaniards quickly adopted the exciting new drink but changed it a little and made it like we do, serving it hot and sweetened – without the chilli peppers! They kept this wonderful discovery a huge secret, protecting it for centuries before the recipe leaked to neighbouring countries like England in the 1700s. Hot chocolate became a big hit in London, where 'chocolate houses' were established to serve the drink. It was the English who started to add milk to the chocolate mixture, making it lighter and more similar to the hot chocolate we enjoy today.

243

Wolf *(cont'd)*

6. Wolf Pack – a group of wolves that lives and plays together, like a family, is called a pack. Packs can be as small as two members, or as big as thirty – but they usually have about six to eight members. Pack life makes it easier for wolves to raise their young and, more importantly, hunt for food.

7. Arctic Wolves – the wolves that live near the North Pole are called Arctic wolves, and they're a little different from the grey wolves that live in warmer environments. These wolves are slightly smaller than their grey relatives, weighing up to 50 kilogrammes and measuring about five feet from the tip of their nose to the tip of their tail. To help reduce heat loss in their chilly surroundings, they have more rounded ears, a shorter muzzle and shorter legs. They also have hair between the pads of their feet to help them walk through the snow.

Arctic wolves' most special feature is the long, thick, snowy white fur that makes them seem to disappear right into their surroundings. These wolves look as if they've been dipped into a pile of pure snow! This perfect camouflage – along with big sharp teeth and a great sense of sight, smell and hearing – makes white wolves excellent hunters. These animals are brave! They run at speeds of up to 35 miles per hour to hunt animals that are many times their size, like the giant musk ox! But there's no need for us to be scared – wolves almost never attack people!

Wombat, *n. (Zoöl.)*
The common name given to the *Phascolomydae*, a family of *Rodentia*, which have large, flat heads, short legs and a body that appears as if crushed. They have coarse brown

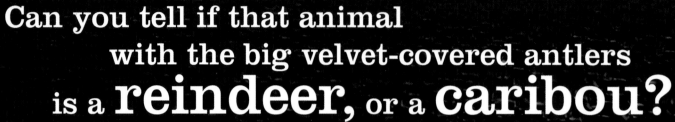

Can you tell if that animal
        with the big velvet-covered antlers
    is a **reindeer**, or a **caribou?**

That's a trick question, because the answer is it's both! In some parts of the world, like Alaska and Canada, people refer to wild reindeer as caribou – but both names describe the same animal.

Reindeer are members of the deer family that have adapted special physical features to live in cold, snowy climates like the Arctic. Each hair in their outer coat is hollow and traps warm air, keeping the reindeer warm – and allowing them to lie down in the snow without melting it! Thick fur even covers their muzzles, which they use to burrow under the deep snow to find their favourite food – lichens called 'reindeer mosses'.

THE POLAR EXPRESS

Reindeer are herbivores, which means they only munch on plants like willow leaves, lichens and small shrubs such as the blueberry. But because these animals are plant eaters, they're always on the move in search of enough food to eat. Reindeer migrate in herds that travel south for the winter and north for the summer. Experts think they have a built-in compass, just like migratory birds, because they can travel through unfamiliar areas to reach the same grounds year after year.

There's a reason Santa chose reindeer to be his special helpers. Aside from being well equipped to make long journeys, these animals are strong and can pull a sledge twice their own weight. With some reindeer weighing as much as 320 kilogrammes, just imagine how many toys they can pull in one go!

Did you know that there are different types of **ice**?

A few types of ice have some pretty strange names; one of these is pancake ice. Pancake ice is thin, very flat, and is the first layer of ice that freezes on top of a body of water. Its name comes from the fact that it lies in pieces across the water's surface, just like separate pancakes sizzling away in a skillet! Growler ice is the name given to small-scale icebergs that make a creepy growling sound when they grind against the hull of a passing ship. These are two of the most common types of ice seen in the Arctic.

This icy tundra is what the **polar bear** calls home.

POLAR BEARS might be one of the largest land mammals alive, but they're also one of the hardest to spot. That's because they're so well camouflaged in the snowy Arctic region, where they live. But I bet you didn't know that polar bears don't really have white fur – every individual hair in a polar bear's coat is actually a hollow tube! Each tube traps the sun's energy and channels the heat to the bear's skin, helping to keep him warm in the icy Arctic climate.

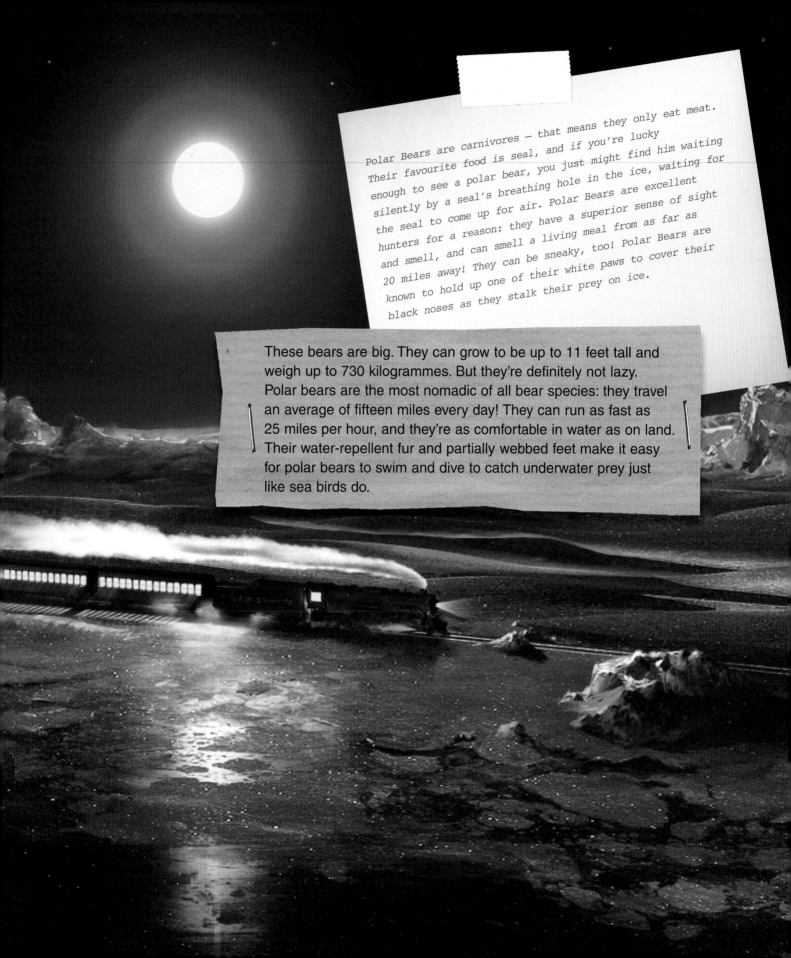

Polar Bears are carnivores — that means they only eat meat. Their favourite food is seal, and if you're lucky enough to see a polar bear, you just might find him waiting silently by a seal's breathing hole in the ice, waiting for the seal to come up for air. Polar Bears are excellent hunters for a reason: they have a superior sense of sight and smell, and can smell a living meal from as far as 20 miles away! They can be sneaky, too! Polar Bears are known to hold up one of their white paws to cover their black noses as they stalk their prey on ice.

These bears are big. They can grow to be up to 11 feet tall and weigh up to 730 kilogrammes. But they're definitely not lazy. Polar bears are the most nomadic of all bear species: they travel an average of fifteen miles every day! They can run as fast as 25 miles per hour, and they're as comfortable in water as on land. Their water-repellent fur and partially webbed feet make it easy for polar bears to swim and dive to catch underwater prey just like sea birds do.

The northern lights
can be as colourful as fireworks!

This colourful display of lights is called the aurora borealis, a natural phenomenon. Auroras occur when energy from the sun interacts with the earth's atmosphere, which is made up of different gases such as oxygen and nitrogen.

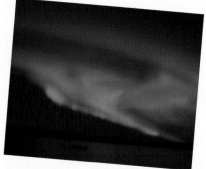

A picture of the NORTHERN LIGHTS, taken on GUNFLINT LAKE in NORTHERN MINNESOTA.

Here's how it works: the sun is constantly giving off charged particles like protons and electrons, forming the solar wind, which travels away from the sun at speeds of about one million miles per hour. When these speedy particles enter the Earth's upper atmosphere, they collide with atoms of atmospheric gases and produce the light that forms auroras.

No two auroras are alike – each has a unique shape, size and colour. The colour of the light created depends on the type of gas that interacts with the solar wind, and no two gases give off exactly the same colours. The most common aurora is made up of a yellow-green light, and it's a result of the solar wind's collision with oxygen at altitudes of about 100 to 300 kilometres. The colour of the aurora can also depend on the height where the solar wind strikes the atmosphere – collisions with those same oxygen atoms at altitudes above 300 kilometres produce rare red auroras.

Why don't you see this display of lights from your back garden? Before the solar wind hits the Earth's atmosphere, it's captured by the Earth's magnetosphere – the region surrounding our planet formed by the Earth's magnetic field. When the charged particles of the solar wind approach the Earth they are drawn to the North or South Pole by the force of this magnetic field before they are able to descend and bump into the atmosphere. That's why the aurora borealis is easily seen at the North Pole, while the South Pole enjoys views of the aurora australis.

MAGNETIC FIELD OF THE EARTH

FIG. 01.

Santa's other airship

Have you ever seen a gigantic blimp fly overhead and wondered how a machine that big could float?

BLIMP.

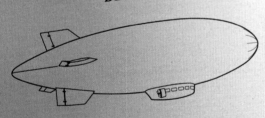

Blimps and zeppelins are both types of airships that are steerable 'lighter-than-air' crafts. What makes a vehicle 'lighter-than-air'? Using a lifting gas, such as helium, the airship becomes lighter than the air surrounding it. For the same reason a piece of wood will float in water, the craft floats in the heavier air – that's why the name airship is so perfect! Lifting gas fills out the fabric envelope structure of an airship and makes the machine

lift, just like a balloon filled with helium! In fact, an airship is a lot like a giant balloon with an engine, so you can 'drive' it through the air instead of having to be carried by the wind.

What's the difference between a blimp and a zeppelin? A zeppelin is called a rigid airship because it has a fixed internal structure that maintains its shape. That structure is covered with a fabric skin. A blimp, however, doesn't have an internal frame. Instead, blimps hold their shape from the pressure of the lifting gas keeping them in the air.

ZEPPELIN.

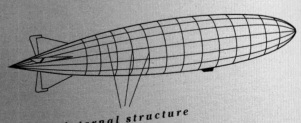

internal structure

What could be better than a great Christmas present, all wrapped up?

MAKE YOUR OWN

How about making your own wrapping paper for the presents that you give to your family and friends? It's fun.

KEEP IT SIMPLE WITH STICKERS.

Brighten up plain paper with whatever stickers you like! Turn red or green wrapping paper into a blizzard of polka dots with differently coloured sticker dots. Or hint at what's inside: teddy bear stickers on a wrapped teddy bear, or train stickers on a toy train set.

Jazz up your wrapping paper using rubber stamps and ink pads. You can make this activity even more fun by creating your own stamps out of sponges. Choose biscuit cutters in snazzy festive shapes like stars, Christmas trees and angels, and then use a thin marker to draw their outlines on some kitchen sponges. Cut out the outlined shapes with scissors, dip in paint and stamp away! Not afraid to get a little messy? Use your own fingertips – or even hands – as stamps!

The **Christmas tree** at the North Pole is one of the most spectacular ever.

THE LEGEND OF THE FIRST CHRISTMAS TREE

In the sixteenth century, a German religious reformer named Martin Luther was walking home one winter's evening near Christmastime. During his stroll, he noticed how beautiful the twinkling stars looked against a background of dark evergreen trees standing tall along his path. He was so awed by the beautiful sight that he decided to recreate the scene for his family. Luther cut down a small evergreen tree and set it up in the sitting room of his home. He attached candles to the tree's branches, lit them, and declared that this would be a symbol of the Christmas sky.

Jingle bells! Jingle bells!

Do you know what kind of bells are on Santa's sleigh? They are crotal bells, and they're one of the dozens of different types of bells in the world. Bells are one of the oldest musical instruments in history — they've been around for more than 5,000 years. Even before they were used to make music (or announce Santa's arrival), people rang bells and even wore bells during dark winter nights, believing they would scare away evil spirits!

SLEIGH BELLS
Crotal bells are closed hollow spheres with a pellet captured inside – kind of like a walnut. The loose pellet – also called a jinglet or pea – is a small ball usually made of metal that rattles about inside the crotal to sound the bell. All it takes is a little movement to make the bell ring; that's why they jingle with every reindeer movement.

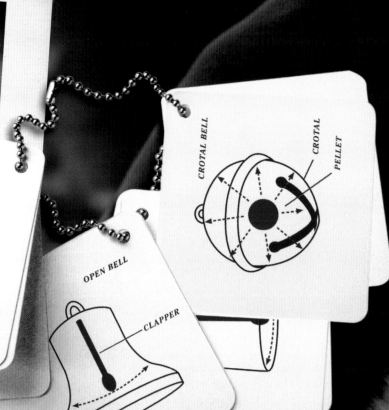

CROTAL BELL

CROTAL PELLET

OPEN BELL

CLAPPER

POLAR POP

POST CARD

PLACE STAMP HERE

The many exciting things the boy saw and learned on his Polar Express journey will live for years to come in his memory and in this scrapbook of his special and extraordinary experiences.

Have you ever made a scrapbook of a memorable time in your life? Why not make your next adventure truly unforgettable by creating your own scrapbook, so that you can relive the excitement every time you open the cover and flip through its pages?

The pictures you include, the things you write about – they're all up to you. Just remember to keep your eyes, ears and mind open – after all, you never know when you will find yourself on a journey you'll never want to forget.